D0949112

GENTLEMEN'S ALLIANCE CROSS

Story & Art by

Arina Tanemura

Vol. 7

CONTENTS

Chapter 28: The Rush of My Heartbeat: Cherry Blossom Gateway 3

Chapter 29: Opening Heart Fantasia 37

Chapter 30: Like Singing a Melody Under Your Breath 71

Chapter 31: Hydrangea Always Bloom in the Rain 105

Chapter 32: Reminiscence, the Canary's Song 139

Bonus Funnies 172

Bonus Story: Maora's Mind Oracle Generation ☆ 174

Notes on the Text 181

【7】
THE GENTLEMEN'S ALLIANCE CROSS
CHAPTER 28: THE RUSH OF MY HEARTBEAT: CHERRY BLOSSOM GATEWAY

CHARACTER INTRODUCTIONS

(Younger Twin)

THE REAL SHIZUMASA
An illness prevents him from attending school. He helped Haine mend her yanki ways.

(Elder Twin)

TAKANARI TOGU
Student Council President
The double. Referred to as "the Emperor" and is the highest authority in school. Wrote Haine's favorite picture book.

▲HAINE OTOMIYA
Bodyguard & General Affairs
A cheerful girl who is in love with Shizumasa-sama. Former juvenile delinquent. Adopted into the Otomiya family in fourth grade.

MAGURI TSUJIMIYA
Vice President
In love with the Emperor.

He appears in the most unexpected places.

Planning Events & Accounting
Childhood friend of Maguri.

USHIO AMAMIYA
Clerk
Haine's friend. Haine is dearer to her than anyone.

Haine Otomiya is a former juvenile delinquent who attends Imperial Academy. One day, she is appointed the rank of "Platinum" as Emperor ShizumasaTogu's fake girlfriend in order to ward off the other girls. Now having found out that there are two Emperors, Haine's heart sways between Shizumasa and Takanari.

The members of the student council performed *Cinderella* for the graduating students, and Haine tried to keep her distance from Takanari. Witnessing this, the Postman revealed who he really is—Maora! Maora then said he would run to become the new Emperor so Haine will become his!

While Takanari considered what was best for the academy during the election, Maora tried to cheat by rigging the votes. Haine found out what Maora was up to and challenged him to a duel! Realizing that Haine was truly worried about him, Maora had a change of heart...

Takanari returns to the position of Emperor, and finally, the student council is back to its usual self again...

IN THE BACK OF MY HEART THERE'S A DOOR...
...UPON WHICH SOMEONE CONTINUES TO KNOCK.
THAT'S THE SOUND I HEAR...
...WHEN I'M WITH YOU...
...BECAUSE I WANT YOU TO HOLD ME TIGHT.

Chapter 28: The Rush of My Heartbeat: Cherry Blossom Gateway

Lead-in My voice and heart are like two opposing mirrors...

This is a one-shot, which is rare for *The Gentleman's Alliance †*. I wrote it because I wanted to draw the Togu mansion.

To differentiate between Shizumasa and Takanari... Well, I try to make Shizumasa look slightly younger, so I draw his eyes larger. (But when I hurry, I end up drawing Takanari's eyes pretty large too...ᵕ̈)

This is one of those chapters where you see Hainekko agonizing over her worries, so I tried drawing her in a mini form in those scenes so that the drawings don't all look the same.

Actually, the bonus story about Kusame and Komaki that was included in volume 5 takes place a little after this chapter, so Kusame and Komaki are not going out yet at this point.

Kusame goes down to the convenience store claiming to get snacks while eating an ice cream. And even after Komaki arrives, he continues to play computer games. I really like the fact that Kusame is an average middle schooler. (laugh)

And his favorite drink is Fanta Grape!!

I'LL BE AT SHIZUMASA-SAMA'S HOUSE!!
SHIZUMASA-SAMA....
I HAVEN'T SEEN HIM FOR QUITE A WHILE NOW.
TAKANARI-SAMA ATTENDS SCHOOL IN HIS PLACE...
...SO IT CAN'T BE HELPED THAT I DON'T GET TO SEE HIM...
TMP
TMP
But...
I'LL BE ABLE TO SEE HIM IF I GO TO HIS HOUSE, WON'T I?!
I'M IN LOVE WITH SHIZUMASA-SAMA!!
BUT...
I'M DRAWN TO TAKANARI-SAMA TOO...
I MUSTN'T THINK ABOUT IT!!
AAAAAAAH!
SWIP
SWIP
SWIP
OPERATION GATECRASH
(The Plan)

GRIP
I'M GOING TO SEE SHIZUMASA-SAMA!!
...TO PLEASE HOLD ME TIGHTLY...
KYAAH
I'm so embarrassed!
I'M GOING TO SEE HIM AND ASK HIM...
I WANT YOU...
...TO FILL UP MY HEART.

Hello.

Tanemura here. Here is volume 7 of the *The Gentleman's Alliance †*.

Hm, this is something a little personal. My longest manga series were *Jeanne* and *Full Moon*, but now *Gentlemen's Alliance* is scheduled to be longer than those two... (Actually, it's already longer.)

And that is all thanks to all you fans who have supported this series, and to the work of all the staff and members of the editorial office.

I'm going to continue working hard on the series, so please support me along with Haine and the others.♥

Now back to volume 7...♪

ARE...
YOU TOLD ME THAT SHIZUMASA-SAMA COULDN'T SEE ME TODAY...
Hmm.
But you let me in.
TMP
TMP
...ARE YOU SURE, KIRIAKI-SAN?
DEEP DOWN, I'M SURE HE WANTS TO SEE YOU.
SHIZUMASA-SAMA REALLY DOES THINK DEARLY OF YOU, HAINE-SAMA.
!
THANK YOU VERY MUCH.

Animal Crossing: Wild World

This is a game for Nintendo DS, and though I happen to be a little lazy, I have been able to drop by the village every day.

By the way, the village is called "Tane Village."

My favorite friend is Blaire-chan (squirrel).♥

I have fun creating Haine-chan's school uniform and whatnot in the game.

It's a lot of fun to see the seasonal changes like the cherry blossom trees blooming and the snow falling.

By the way, my room is in the classical theme, and my second floor has black and white furniture with a wallpaper night scene to give it a urbanized look.

Arina from Tane Village

A young girl who like to change shoes. I like the boots.♥

I THOUGH KIRIAKI-SAN WAS A LITTLE SCARY...

...BUT HE SEEMS REALLY KIND... WHEN HE'S TALKING ABOUT SHIZUMASA-SAMA.

WELL, HE IS SHIZUMASA-SAMA'S PERSONAL ATTENDANT.

Like Toya-kun is for Takanari-sama.

TOYA-KUN! ♪

WHAT ARE YOU STARING AT?

Hello there! ♥

KIRIAKI... WATER!
KOFF
KOFF
KOFF
KIRIAKI!
I caught a fish.
Praise me!
MEW
A STRAY CAT WITH A FISH IN ITS MOUTH...
HA HA.☆ YOU EACH TREAT OTOMIYA-KUN AS YOUR MASTER'S PREY, DON'T YOU?!
RWAR
Woo hoo!
KIRIAKI!
WATER...
HERE YOU ARE.
!

HAINE...!
GLARE!!
KIRIAKI!!
GWAR
WHY'D YOU LET HAINE IN?!!
PLEASE FORGIVE ME!!
ARGH!
BUT YOU KEPT MUTTERING HAINE-SAMA'S NAME IN YOUR SLEEP...
SHUT UP!
...SO I TOOK THE LIBERTY OF INVITING HER INSIDE!!
Shi...
Shizumasa-sama.
Don't get too angry— your fever...

KA-CHAK
I'll be outside.
IT WAS MY FAULT. I TOLD HIM TO LET ME IN...
I'M SORRY, SHIZUMASA-SAMA!
DON'T BE ANGRY AT KIRIAKI-SAN!
I MUST LOOK TERRIBLE TO YOU...
...LIKE THIS...
IT'S NOT YOU.
THAT'S NOT THE REASON...
?

I REALLY WANTED TO SEE YOU...
...HAINE.
SHIZUMASA-SAMA!!
"PLEASE HOLD ME TIGHT."
WOULD IT BE OKAY...
BUT...
...TO ASK YOU THAT?
BUT...
ME TOO!
I REALLY WANTED TO SEE YOU TOO!!

I...
HAINE.
PLEASE...!!
HAINE?
JOLT
IT'S NOTHING.
IT'S NOTHING AT ALL.
NO...

HAGGARD
I COULDN'T ASK HIM!
Please come again!
Why did I come here then?
HOW STUPID COULD I BE?!
I'M AN IDIOT!!
I'M GOING TO GO HOME AND MAKE KOMAKI AND KUSAME COMFORT ME.
WAAH
OH
COUPLE
CLOG
LONER
PITIFUL
HISSS
I don't know why...
...but I feel so miserable!
HEY.

HISS
WHAT ARE YOU DOING?
TAKANARI-SAMA!!
Needless to say, Toya told him, and he came after her.
WHAT ARE YOU DOING HERE?!
ARE YOU LEAVING?
I'LL WALK YOU HOME.
!!
B-BMP

NO...!
TH-THAT'S OKAY!!
I CAN GO HOME ALONE!!
UH...
TMP TMP TMP TMP
FORK IN THE ROAD
PLEASE WALK ME HOME...
SIGH
OKAY.
Um. Um. Um. Um.
This way? That way? Which way?

I SHOULDN'T GET TOO CLOSE TO HIM.
TMP
TMP
TMP
COME TO THINK OF IT...
THIS IS THE FIRST TIME WE'VE WALKED ALONE TOGETHER SINCE THAT DATE...
I LOVE YOU...!!
B-BMP
STRANGE...
AHH! I DIDN'T KNOW ABOUT THE TWINS BACK THEN...
...BUT I CAN'T FORGIVE MYSELF FOR BEING SO CLOSE TO SOMEBODY OTHER THAN SHIZUMASA-SAMA!!
AHHHHHHH

AHH! I MUSTN'T THINK ABOUT IT!!
HAINE, YOU FICKLE GIRL!! YANKI!! CINDERELLA!!
IN A PANIC
?
HAINE.
LOOK UP.
WHEN WE WALK, THE DISTANCE BETWEEN US HAS GROWN BIGGER...
...BUT YOU FEEL SO MUCH CLOSER THAN BEFORE.

OH...
THE CHERRY BLOSSOMS ARE BEAUTIFUL!
We're in the park, right?
THEY'RE SO CUTE...
Why do girls always say things are "cute"?
THE NEW TERM STARTS SOON.
YES.
AND WE'LL HEAR YOUR ORIENTATION SPEECH!
I'LL BE COUNTING ON YOU FOR GUIDANCE EVEN NOW THAT I'M A SECOND-YEAR, EMPEROR!

B-B-MP
GRIP
SURE.
HAINE...
...I WANT YOU TO HAVE THIS.

HUH?
IT'S... MY TREASURE.
Ahhh!
I-I CAN'T ACCEPT IT!!
SHE TOOK IT FROM HIM WITHOUT THINKING
IT'S NOT EXPENSIVE OR ANY-THING.
I JUST WANT YOU TO KEEP IT, HAINE.
WHAT'S THAT SUPPOSED TO MEAN ?!
THEN I REALLY SHOULDN'T ACCEPT IT!
YOU DON'T HAVE TO LOOK INSIDE.
Just take it.
I—
BUT...

HEH
HEH
HEH
HEH
HEH
HEH
WIP
WIP
AHH! EMBAR-RASSING!
WIP
THWIP
ZINGE
FWAT
HERE, GIVE ME YOUR HAND.
OKAY...
OH...

HUG

LET ME GO...
YOU MUSTN'T!
I...
TA...
TAKANARI-SAMA....!
TAKANARI-SAMA, YOU MUSTN'T...!!
I LOVE YOU SO MUCH...
WHY WON'T YOU BE MINE?

JUP
BLUSH
I MUSTN'T?
BUT YOU'RE NOT TELLING ME NO?
PLEASE...
...STOP THIS!

B-BMP
B-BMP
B-BMP
B-BMP
IN THE BACK OF MY HEART THERE'S A DOOR...
...UPON WHICH SOMEONE CONTINUES TO KNOCK.
B-BMP
B-BMP
THAT'S THE... SOUND I HEAR...
B-BMP
B-BMP

KA-CHAK
NEE-SAMA, WELCOME HOME!
KUSAME WAS JUST TEACHING ME HOW TO PLAY A COMPUTER GAME.
WHY DON'T YOU JOIN US?
WHAT'S THE MATTER, NEE-SAMA?!
YOUR FACE IS ALL RED!!
A COMPLEX KIND OF JEALOUSY
HUH?!
DO YOU HAVE A FEVER?

B-BMP
KUSAME, LEND ME A HAND.
HELP ME TAKE NEE-SAMA TO HER ROOM.
HUH, ME?!
YES, YOU!!
Why are you embarrassed?
B-BMP
B-BMP
WHO KEEPS...
...KNOCKING ON THE DOOR TO MY HEART SO PASSIONATELY?
B-BMP
B-BMP

TAKANARI-SAMA?
SHIZUMASA-SAMA?

IT'S NEITHER. IT'S JUST MY FEELINGS...
...PRESSING ME TO TELL HIM...
...THAT I DIDN'T MEAN WHAT I SAID.

TAKANARI-SAMA...
I WANTED YOU TO HOLD ME...
CHAPTER 28/END

THE GENTLEMEN'S ALLIANCE CROSS
POPULARITY POLL: CHARACTER SURVEYS
2
They are going
I'm Komaki!
I'm sister ne cute Kindly aine sama...
† NAME OF THE PERSON YOU'RE VOTING FOR:
Haine Otomiya-sama
† WHAT YOU LIKE ABOUT THAT PERSON:
She's so kind! And so cute!
Then it
KOMAKI KAMIYA
In the face of ethics allegations involving his administration
† NAME OF THE PERSON YOU'RE VOTING FOR:
Haine otomiya-sama
† WHAT YOU LIKE ABOUT THAT PERSON:
Her kind, easygoing ways.
yers
TACHIBANA KAMIYA
Hahn defends his integrity
I intend to work hard with all your cheers and love supporting me.
How do you do, my name is Tachibana Kamiya.
That stars
listed on the ballot as James Kenneth Hahn but little of his father's personality.
Governmental Studies, a nonpartisan research group in Los Angeles.
"People need to have an image of where.

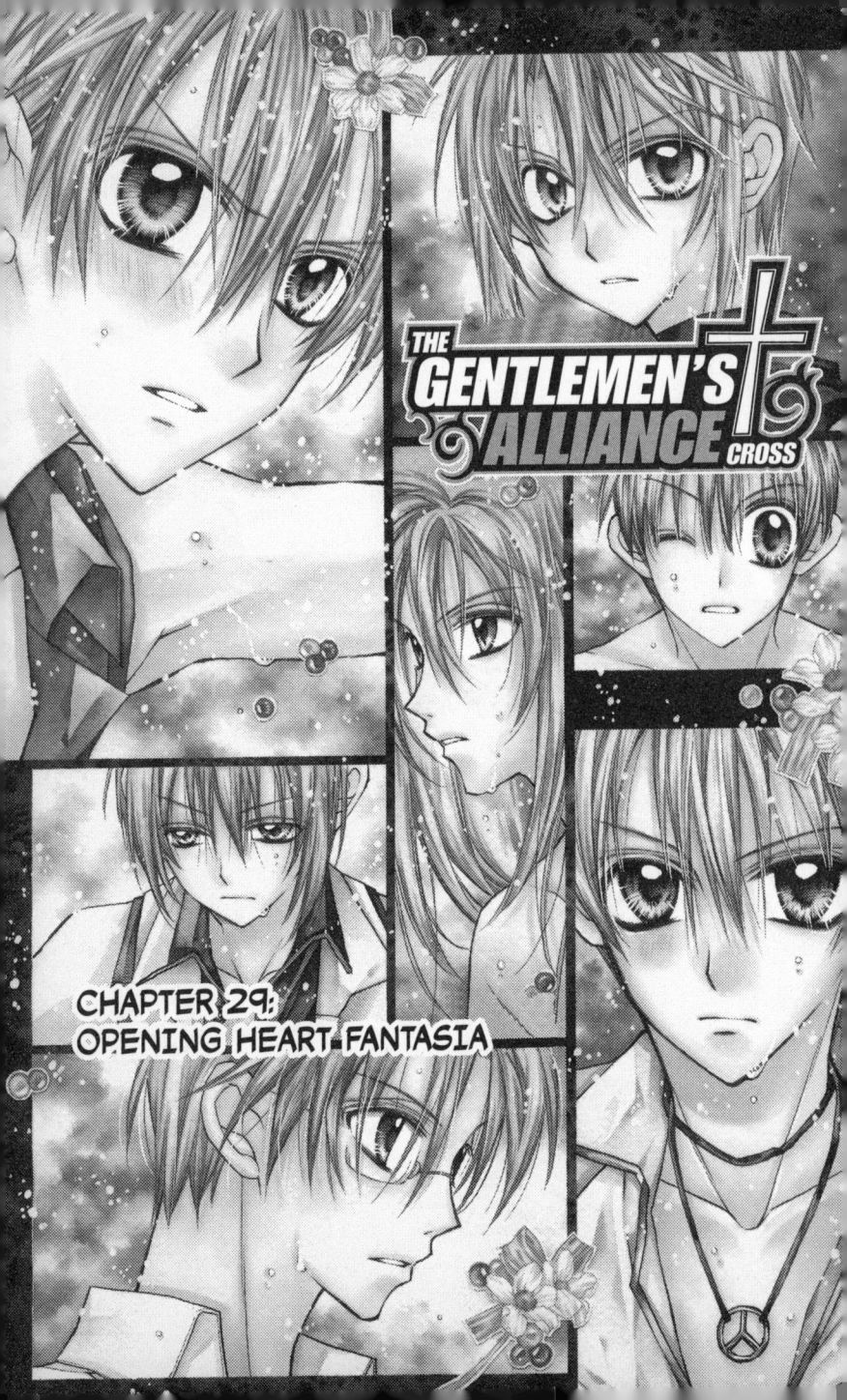
THE GENTLEMEN'S ALLIANCE CROSS
CHAPTER 29:
OPENING HEART FANTASIA

I'm Kusame's friend, Mizuki.
Nice to meet you, ladies.
I appear only in the bonus story...
† NAME OF THE PERSON YOU'RE VOTING FOR:
KOMAKI KAMIYA
† WHAT YOU LIKE ABOUT THAT PERSON:
HER RAPID MOOD CHANGES.
SHE'S SO CUTE!
MIZUKI KOTOMIYA
† NAME OF THE PERSON YOU'RE VOTING FOR:
KOMAKI
† WHAT YOU LIKE ABOUT THAT PERSON:
SHE'S CUTE.
SHE WATCHED HIM WRITE IT..
Nice to meet you... Hey, why do I have to write something like this?
I'm Kusame Otomiya.
KUSAME OTOMIYA

Chapter 29: Opening Heart Fantasia

Lead-in This fever is your fault...

Spoilers! I'm giving away the story!

In this chapter I challenged myself to draw a dream—an incomprehensible dream. And yes, it turned out to be pretty hard work...(laugh) My blood type is A (though I don't know if that has anything to do with this), so my ideas tend to be sensible. They don't turn out to be as surreal as I would wish them to be...

Sorry, I really don't know if having blood-type A has anything do with this or not.

In the chapter in which Haine was kidnapped, I drew Maora, Maguri, and Ushio as pigs—and I liked the pigs a lot. I decided to draw them as pigs again. The latter half of the dream is probably Haine's wish that everything would be so peaceful if it was like this...

Also, the kiss scene at the end, well... "The girl kissing the guy" is taboo for me. I know it's silly, but it happens to be a no-no in my manga series...

But I'm trying to break my personal taboos in *The Gentlemen's Alliance †!* So I gave it a try... Well, I tried to stop her, but Haine wouldn't listen...(laugh) I wanted to focus on Haine's inner battle in this chapter. (The last line is supposed to express how she's surrendered to her feelings.)

WE'RE NOW SECOND-YEAR STUDENTS!!
...THAT'S THAT! HERE COMES SPRING!!
THE START OF A NEW TERM.
KYAAAH! IT'S THE MEMBERS OF THE STUDENT COUNCIL!
FIRST YEARS
PLEASE SIGN THIS FOR ME!

PSST
THEY'RE ALL SO POPULAR, AREN'T THEY?
KYAAH
KYAAH
Eh?
I'VE HEARD THAT THE CURRENT STUDENT COUNCIL IS THE MOST POPULAR IN SCHOOL HISTORY.
THEY'RE LIKE IDOLS.
SLINK
OOOOH! IT'S HAINE-SAMA!!
IT'S HAINE-SAMA, THE PLATINUM!!
It must be because the Emperor is such a wonderful person.
The one and only!
The one and only?!
JOLT
BAHA HA
Haine-sama is so cute!
HA HA
WHY ARE YOU ALL...
...LAUGHING AT ME?!
HA HA HA HA
HA HA
STARTING TODAY, THERE'S A STUDENT ORIENTATION THAT LASTS THREE DAYS AND TWO NIGHTS.
We startled her!

THE STUDENT COUNCIL WILL ATTEND...
...SO OFF WE GO TO THE MOUNTAINS OF HAKONE!!
Haine-sama, may I shake your hand?
Sure.
GRR
GRR
GRR
GRR
GRR
NEW STUDENT ORIENTATION: ROOM ASSIGNMENTS
NAME
TOYA
USHIO AMAMIYA
NAME
MAGURI TSUJIMI
WHAT IS THIS?!
SHUT UP!
I'M GOING TO HANG OUT WITH USHIO-CHAN...
WHY?
IN CHARGE OF ROOM ASSIGNMENTS
It's too sad!!
Get off me
HOW COME MAORA AND I ARE IN DIFFERENT ROOMS?!!

?
You're so cute, Maguri!
OF COURSE HE WOULD!
AFTER ALL, THEY ARE GOING OUT.
They're in love.
MAGURI WANTS TO BE IN THE SAME ROOM AS MAORA? THAT'S RARE.
SILENCE
SHI...
...SHIZUN?
...Maora's tie?
You didn't notice...
PANG
MAGURI...
...WE'LL STILL BE TOGETHER, RIGHT?
...EVEN THOUGH YOU HAVE A LOVER NOW...
B-B
MOE MOE
M
P
PANT PANT

OF COURSE!! ACTUALLY...
SHIZUN, I STILL—
THUD
MAGURI IS ROOMING WITH TOYA-KUN... AND MAO-CHAN IS WITH USHIO...
One. Two.
HUH?
Three.
Maguri, my friend
SO THAT MEANS...
SHUP
SHUP
SHUP
SHUP

THE EMPEROR AND THE PLATINUM...
...ARE SHARING A ROOM.
PSST
THERE'S ONLY ONE BED.
CARRYING LUGGAGE
GWAR
T-TOYA-KUN, YOU'VE REALLY GONE TOO FAR THIS TIME!!
HUH?! OH, NO! IT WASN'T ME! IT WASN'T ME!
Things just turned out this way.
STRAY CAT.
Grah!
PREY
THAT'S NOT THE POINT!!
BUT DON'T WORRY.
I WON'T TELL SHIZUMASA-SAMA.

Hmm.
...
I'll leave you two now...
KA-CHAK
I'M SLEEPING IN USHIO'S ROOM!!
UGH.
FIRST RUMOR: "THE EMPEROR AND PLATINUM ARE ON BAD TERMS."
PSST
HE'S COMING UP WITH HEADLINES FOR THE SCHOOL NEWSPAPER!
THEN: "A BREAKUP IS CLOSE AT HAND..."
NEXT: "A SUDDEN TURN OF EVENTS AFTER THE EMPEROR ELECTION..."
PSST
PSST
PSST
ALL RIGHT.
I'LL SLEEP ON THE SOFA.
KA-CHAK
HUH?

WE'RE ALONE.
SHIZUMASA ISN'T HERE.
WITH YOU THIS CLOSE TO ME...
...HOW CAN I HOLD MYSELF BACK THROUGH THE NIGHT?

TONIGHT...
...I'LL MAKE YOU MINE.
KA-CHAK

WHAT SHOULD I DO NOW?
NO...
NO...
B-BMP
B-BMP
B-BMP
HEE
HEE
HEE
SHFF
SHFF
PERFECT!!
POP

GLARE
OOH!
THE EXPRESSION ON NEE-SAMA'S FACE THE OTHER DAY... SHE MUST BE LOVESICK!!
I'm sure of it!!
WE MUST DO SOME-THING!!
THERE ARE TOO MANY ATTENDANTS AROUND THE EMPEROR FOR HIM TO LOOSEN UP!
I'M SURE HE'LL BE ABLE TO HAVE A LONG TALK WITH NEE-SAMA IF WE GET THEM ALONE!!
BLUSH BLUSH
HOW BEAUTIFUL IT IS TO BE SO DEVOTED TO ONE'S SISTER!!
BUT YOU DIDN'T HAVE TO GO SO FAR AS TO ASK MAORA-SAMA TO PUT THEM IN THE SAME ROOM...
THEY FOLLOWED HAINE EVEN THOUGH THEY AREN'T SUPPOSED TO BE HERE
Nee-sama!
Go!! Go!!
Show him your pretty smile!
Woo hoo!
WE'RE ALONE TOO...
I bet she doesn't even know what it means for a guy and a girl to be alone together at night!
HMPH
Such a princess!

★KamiKaze Kaito Jeanne

My second manga series, *KamiKaze Kaito Jeanne* will be published in a collector's edition in Japan!

It will be six volumes total. They will have newly drawn covers, illustrations, and an essay manga!

The final volume will include a bonus story!

We're also planning a little gift for the readers.♥

By the way, the bonus story will probably take place after the main story. It will be about Shinji and Natsuki.

It's been a while since I drew Maroyan!!

Please look forward to it.♥♥♥

HAINE AND I ARE FRIENDS...
I'M NOT LIKE YOU.
HUH?
WHAT BOYFRIEND ?!
I'M GOING TO SLEEP IN MY BOYFRIEND'S ROOM TONIGHT.
LIAR!!
I'm going to take a shower.
Gehh!
I ADVISE TO YOU STOP BEING EMBARRASSED AND ASK MAGURI OVER.
Maguri still avoids telling me that he loves me...
NO WAY.
SULK

Special Thanks♪

Nakame Saori

Meech
Yuko-chan
Chihiro-chan
Ooka-san

Hina-chan
Ibuki-chan
Sakura-chan
Toma-chan
Negami-san
Kona-chan

Asa-chan

Riku & Kai

Ribon Editorial Department
Shueisha

Ammonite Ltd

IN THE BATH-ROOM
GO SLEEP BY YOURSELF!
I WON'T DO ANY-THING!
...
FULLY
NO!
NEVER!
JUST HAD A BATH TOO
ARMED
PROMISE?
...
SEE!!
I can't promise.
GRAH
I GUESS YOU REALLY DON'T LIKE ME...

THAT'S NOT IT...
THAT'S NOT IT...
BUT...

WHY WON'T THINGS WORK OUT IN THIS WORLD?
HUH?
FLOAT
FLOAT
WHERE AM I?
I'M HOLDING AN ENVELOPE.
TUP
WHY...?
OINK
KLAP KLAP KLAP
KLAP KLAP KLAP
KLAP KLAP KLAP
1
2
3
SHOCK
?!
?!
?!
WHAT ARE YOU DOING?!
Three pigs?!
I WON! I WON!
HOP
HOP
MEDAL!
POIT

GLINT
GLINT
GLINT
GLINT
GLINT
AH!
AAAH, OKAY! WAIT A MINUTE!!
I'M HUNGRY NOW THAT I'VE WON.
HUNGRY!
SFFT SFFT
SOB
OINK
OINK
POIT
FWAAASH
The scenery changed?
KLIK
Ah! Bright!
BINGO.
THIS IS...
...THE HANGING GARDEN?
I WANT YOU TO FIND THE EMPEROR.
OINK
OINK

UM, I...
SHIZUMASA-SAMA...?
KREEE

LONG TIME NO SEE.
HAINE!
YOU'RE NOT SHIZUMASA-SAMA.
HUH?
WHAT ARE YOU TALKING ABOUT? I'M SHIZUMASA TOGU.
I'M AN ONLY CHILD... ♪
I see.
...AND THE EMPEROR.
THE NEXT LINE...
...IS YOURS.
HAVE YOU FORGOTTEN IT?
OH...

YOU...
...YOU SHOULD FALL IN LOVE WITH ME!
IS IT OKAY...
...TO FALL IN LOVE WITH YOU?

YES...!
AND THIS...
...IS SUCH A HAPPY STORY.

Hm?
SLEEPY
OH.
I WAS DREAMING.
HUH?
WHAT HAPPENED IN MY DREAM?
Um, medals...
And they were hungry...
CHAK

I THINK I'VE SEEN...
...HIS SLEEPING FACE BEFORE...
TAKANARI-SAMA.
YOU SHOULD BE...
...SLEEPING IN THE BED.
IT'S SO BEAUTIFUL.
REALLY BEAUTIFUL.
TIME STOPS, AND I CAN'T TAKE MY EYES OFF HIM.

TAKANARI-SAMA.
NO.
...STOP...
NO...
IT'LL TAKE ME PRISONER.
I MUSTN'T LOOK.
TAKANARI-SAMA.
THE ARMS THAT HELD ME...
...ARE EMPTY.
I LOVE SHIZUMASA-SAMA.
IF YOU TOUCH ME...
NO.
...I WON'T BE ABLE TO REFUSE YOU.
I...
BUT I CAN'T...

TAKANARI-SAMA.
TAKANARI-SAMA.
TAKANARI-SAMA.
I CAN'T...
...RESIST...
TAKANARI-SAMA.
TAKANARI-SAMA.

Growers Council has mounted Kodak had violated seven of of fats and oils in fi
an information campaign and Polaroid's key patents on in- ucts in the last year

?!
WHAT JUST HAPPENED?
...AND OPENED THE DOOR MYSELF...
I WAS TEMPTED BY THE DREAM...

† NAME OF THE PERSON YOU'RE VOTING FOR:
Haine Otomiya
† WHAT YOU LIKE ABOUT THAT PERSON:
Everything....
TOGU SHIZUMASA
...
ALL HE WANTS IS JUST ONE VOTE...FROM HAINE.
TOGU SHIZUMASA
† NAME OF THE PERSON YOU'RE VOTING FOR:
Shizumasa Togu-sama
† WHAT YOU LIKE ABOUT THAT PERSON:
I'm extremely happy to see him grow up to become a fine gentleman.
By the way, please don't enter me into the popularity vote without telling me.
I'm Kiriaki. I'm Shizumasa-sama's manservant.
KIRIAKI
† NAME OF THE PERSON YOU'RE VOTING FOR:
TAKANARI TOGU-SAMA
† WHAT YOU LIKE ABOUT THAT PERSON:
EVERYTHING ABOUT HIM IS JUST WONDERFUL.
All my votes are for Takanari-sama.
I'm Toya.
TOYA

CHAPTER 30: LIKE SINGING A MELODY UNDER YOUR BREATH

† NAME OF THE PERSON YOU'RE VOTING FOR:
Ryokka-san (my wife)
† WHAT YOU LIKE ABOUT THAT PERSON:
Everything!
Absolutely!
...So, um... I'm sorry!!
My name is Itsuki Otomiya. I-I have a wife I love, and children...
ITSUKI OTOMIYA
I'm Ryokka. I'm Haine-chan's and Kusame's mother.
My hobby is knitting, and I love to cook.
† NAME OF THE PERSON YOU'RE VOTING FOR:
Maika-sama
† WHAT YOU LIKE ABOUT THAT PERSON:
She's my idol.
RYOKKA OTOMIYA

WHAT DID I JUST DO...?
HAINE...
JUST NOW...
...DID YOU...
BLUSH
...KISS ME?

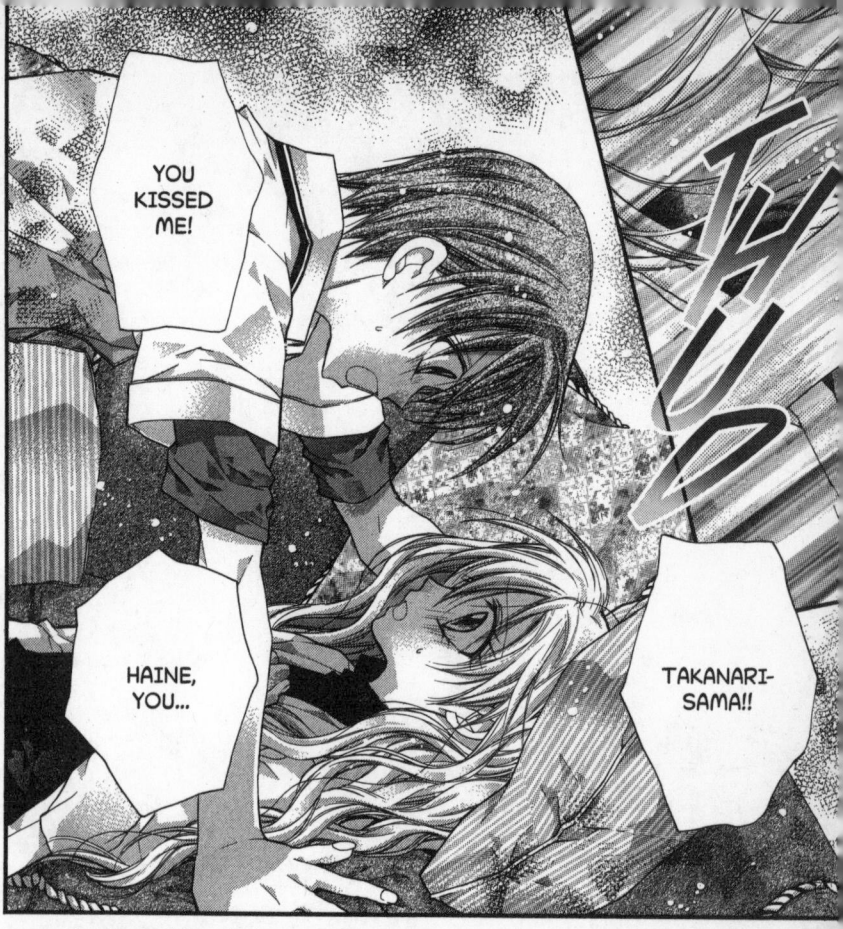

Chapter 30: Like Singing a Melody Under Your Breath

Lead-in The kiss of a couple in love has the power to make stars rain down upon them...!

I'm giving away the story!

I entrusted the lead-in to my supervisor for this chapter. (It's very spirited and cute.) This chapter is very lovey-dovey, isn't it? I had a question from my readers about Maora's "I wouldn't have stopped" line: Did he mean he wouldn't stop if he was in a situation like that with Maguri, or that he wouldn't stop even if Haine-chan asked him to stop? The answer is the latter, by the way.

He basically meant that even if Haine-chan asked him to stop he wouldn't be able to because she's so cute. (laugh)

And also, just making Komaki appear in a scene really adds color to the page. To tell you the truth, it's pretty tough to paint her hair using a brush, but after the result of the popularity vote (I'll have the details in volume 8), I've become more careful in painting it.

Ushio slept over at Senri-sensei's place. I wonder how far these two have gone...? B-BMP B-BMP I think they don't have much of a relationship yet. I have a feeling that Senri would actually ward her off by saying, "I am the school doctor, you know" or something of that sort.

KISSED ME...
!!
TA...
TAKANARI-SAMA!!
TONIGHT...
...I'LL MAKE YOU MINE.
WAI—
NN...
WHAT SHOULD I DO?! WHAT SHOULD I DO?!
I CAN'T BREAK FREE!!
...

I MISTOOK YOU...
...FOR SHIZUMASA-SAMA!
JOLT
MISTOOK ME...?
YOU LOOKED SO MUCH LIKE HIM ASLEEP!
I BEGAN TO THINK THAT YOU WERE ACTUALLY SHIZUMASA-SAMA!
SO I...
...COULDN'T HELP IT!
WUP

OH...
SWIP
SO YOU "MISTOOK" ME FOR SHIZUMASA...
THAT'S...
...THE ONE THING I NEVER WANTED TO HEAR FROM YOU.

KA-CHAK
YOU TWO HAD A FIGHT ?!
DAY 2: HIKING
YEAH.
I CAN'T TELL THEM THE TRUTH, SO...
Um.
IT WAS ALL SO SUDDEN— IT SURPRISED ME.
SO I ENDED UP SAYING SOMETHING REALLY MEAN TO HIM.
KYAAH!
HAINE-CHAN, YOU'RE SO CUTE!!! ♡
YOU MUST'VE BEEN SCARED.
UHH...
I'll hug you. ♡

Hello.

So the cover illustration for the next volume will be of the character who got first place in the popularity vote.

This is to show my gratitude to all the fans who voted. And it's a treat for getting first place. (A treat for that character, that is.)

I can't wait. ♥♥

I'm really busy with both *Jeanne* and *The Gentlemen's Alliance †*, but I'll do my best, so I hope I see you all in the next volume!!

What is this...
Takuto is getting fatter and fatter...
(But the real mystery is that his human form doesn't gain any weight...)

The schedule... was really tight this time, so I'm sorry I couldn't write a lot...

Next time!!
I'll try to include more extra bits and pieces. ♥

BLUSH
BLUSH
BLUSH
BLUSH
BLUSH
BLUSH
REEEALLY?! I WOULDN'T HAVE STOPPED.
I'd press on...
COULD YOU GUYS TALK ABOUT THINGS LIKE THAT IN SECRET, AWAY FROM ME?
...JUST SAYING SO CAN HELP TOO, YOU KNOW. ☆
WHEN YOU CAN'T EXPLAIN SOME-THING....
I'm running away now.
Wait for me Shizun!
...SO YOU'LL HAVE TO THINK ABOUT IT TOGETHER.
THIS INVOLVES YOU TWO...

I have a blog.

http://rikukai.arina.lolipop.jp/

Arina Nikki

MM Boys

SFFT

SFFT

HAINE-CHAN, WE'RE SUPPOSED TO HAVE LUNCH HERE.

TOGETHER...?

Oh, okay.

THE STALKERS

OUTSIDE ALL NIGHT... ...ON A MOUNTAIN...

I PLANNED TO KEEP A WATCH ON NEE-SAMA, BUT I FELL ASLEEP...

I CAN'T BELIEVE HOW CARELESS I WAS!

ARGH!

NEVER!!! ARGH!

LET'S JUST GO HOME BEFORE OUR COLDS GET WORSE.

KOFF

HAVEN'T YOU HAD ENOUGH, KOMAKI?

LUNCHTIME: 11:30
WELL?
MAORA.
WHICH DO YOU WANT—THE SANDWICH OR THE RICE BALL?
SQUEEZE
Sandwich
THERE'S ALSO TEA OR WATER. WHICH DO YOU WANT?
Mmm. ♡
GLOM
GLOM
GLOM
MAORA...
GLOM
HMPH
GRAAH
AND HOW MANY TIMES DO I HAVE TO TELL YOU NOT TO GROPE ME IN PUBLIC?!
JUST ANSWER ME, DAMN IT!!
I KNOW YOU LIKE IT.
RWAR

!!
OOH
"REEEALLY?! I WOULDN'T HAVE STOPPED."
"I'd press on..."
I...
...WON'T STOP EITHER.

SHOVE
OH!!
SHH... LOWER YOUR VOICE.
MAORA!
Just accept me!
WHAT A NAUGHTY GIRL.
WHAT ABOUT YOU, SENSEI?
I'M SURE THERE'S A SICK STUDENT LOOKING FOR YOU.
SHOULDN'T YOU BE INTERACTING WITH ALL THE FRESHMEN?

THEN I GUESS...
...WE'RE PARTNERS IN CRIME.
DON'T...
NO KISSING.
STOP.

I HAVEN'T KISSED ANYONE YET...
WHY?
...
SO...
REALLY?
HOW EXCITING.
PERVERT.

...
...
BLUSH
TMP TMP TMP
HUFF HUFF
EHHH?! IS IT TRUE? COULD THOSE TWO POSSIBLY BE...
...IN A RELATIONSHIP?!
!
COME TO THINK OF IT, LAST NIGHT USHIO-CHAN DID SAY THAT SHE WAS GOING TO SLEEP IN HER BOYFRIEND'S ROOM—AND SHE NEVER CAME BACK!
SO SHE MEANT SENRI-SENSEI...

I DON'T BELIEVE IT.
REALLY?
WHO, ME?
HUH?
MAGURI-KUN... YOU'RE HIDING SOMETHING FROM ME, AREN'T YOU?
TELL ME!
WHAT DO YOU KNOW!!
AND WHY DO YOU KNOW?!
I DON'T KNOW! I DON'T!!
I DON'T KNOW A THING!!
GEH!
You leave me no choice!!
MIND ORACLE GENERATION!!
SHUM

TWINKLE
CHANGED CLOTHES INSTANTLY
PLEASE...
...MAGURI-KUN.
TELL ME!
BLUSH
KRAK
STUPID FLIRT!
Why?
Idiot! Idiot!
GEHHH
THEY'RE BOTH YOU, RIGHT?!

WHERE DID EVERY-ONE...
...DISAPPEAR TO?
The sky is so blue!
ALONE
THIS IS REALLY AWKWARD!!
TAKA... EMPEROR!
Um.
WHICH DO YOU WANT— THE RICE BALL OR THE SANDWICH?
JUST BE CASUAL!
I'M NOT HUNGRY.
...
ALOOF

ALOOF
...
WHATEVER.
I-I THINK I'LL GO AHEAD AND HAVE THE RICE BALL, OKAY?
HE'S STILL ANGRY...
NIBBLE
I CAN'T BLAME HIM.
BUT...
...IF I TOLD YOU THE TRUTH...
...
I'M AFRAID I MIGHT HURT YOU EVEN MORE.

SHFF SHFF
HUH?
W-we're alive...
Oh!
KOMAKI!
KUSAME!!
WHAT ARE YOU DOING HERE?!
GLINT
Refresh Cooling Gel
WHAT A COINCIDENCE, NEE-SAMA!!
TMP TMP TMP
HA HA HA HA
SECRET ASSIGNMENTS MUST BE CARRIED OUT IN SECRET!!
AND...WHY ARE YOU RUNNING AWAY?!
WE'RE ALSO HAVING A SECRET MEETING FOR THE STUDENT COUNCIL!!
GLINT
AT A PLACE LIKE THIS?!
Run for it, Kusame!

FWOOM
SHMM
KOMAKI!!
!!

?!
NOOOOO!!

NEE-SAMA!
SOB SOB
WHAT'S WRONG, KOMAKI?!
WHERE'S HAINE?!
NEE-SAMA!
SHE FELL DOWN THE CLIFF...
NEE-SAMA!
...WHEN SHE STOPPED MY FALL!!

IT'S ALL MY FAULT.
MY FAULT!!
KLATT
STOP CRYING!!
JOLT
WH-WHAT ABOUT YOU, SHIZUN?!
Please come with me, everyone.
MAGURI AND THE OTHERS WILL GATHER PEOPLE WHO ARE FAMILIAR WITH THIS MOUNTAIN!!
I'LL GO LOOK FOR HAINE. I'LL MEET YOU AT THE BOTTOM.
SHMM
KOMAKI, I NEED YOU TO LEAD THE FRESHMEN BACK TO THE LODGING AND WAIT THERE!!
NARIMIYA-SENSEI, YOU CALL FOR AN AMBULANCE!!

SHE'S MY PLATINUM!
I CAN'T LEAVE HER DOWN THERE ALONE !!
SHIZUN...
PLIP
PLIP

BUT... I...
TAKANARI-SAMA, I'M SORRY...
I NEVER KNEW...
HAINE!
MY WAVERING HEART WAS UNABLE TO FULLY ACCEPT YOUR FEELINGS FOR ME...
...HOW HARD IT WAS...
...AND I'VE DONE NOTHING BUT HURT YOU...
...TO BE LOVED.
HAINE!

...
TAKANARI-SAMA...
...TRIED TO SAVE KOMAKI...
...BUT FELL INSTEAD...
I...
CAN YOU SIT UP?
YOU FELL QUITE A LONG WAY, YOU KNOW.
I'M GLAD YOU'RE AWAKE.
DOES YOUR HEAD HURT?
IT'S STARTED TO RAIN...
I REMEMBER.
LET'S MOVE UNDER A TREE.

TAKANARI-SAMA...
YOU WERE SO ANGRY, BUT YOU STILL CAME...
...TO HELP ME.
HELP IS NEAR...
...SO DON'T WORRY.
WHEN YOU CAN'T EXPLAIN SOME-THING...
...JUST SAYING SO...
...CAN HELP TOO, YOU KNOW.

I'M SORRY ABOUT THIS MORNING.
I SHOULDN'T HAVE GOTTEN SO MAD...
...ABOUT THAT.
BUT I LOVE YOU, HAINE.
I JUST COULDN'T LET IT PASS.
YOU'RE THE ONLY PERSON APART FROM THE PEOPLE IN THE TOGU HOUSEHOLD...
...WHO KNOWS I'M "TAKANARI"...

TAKANARI-SAMA.
YEAH.
I SAID I MISTOOK YOU FOR SHIZUMASA-SAMA...
...BUT THAT WAS A LIE.
HAINE?
...
IT...
IT WASN'T LIKE THAT.
I UNDER-STAND.
YOU WERE IN A DAZE JUST NOW, BUT YOU STILL KNEW WHO I WAS.
WHY ARE YOU SO KIND?
I CAN'T HOLD BACK MY FEELINGS FOR YOU...
HAINE...
...DID YOU LIE TO ME?
WHY...

BECAUSE I LOVE YOU...
...TAKANARI-SAMA.
CHAPTER 30 / END

Maika Kamiya
DAZED
MAIKA KAMIYA
† NAME OF THE PERSON YOU'RE VOTING FOR:
† WHAT YOU LIKE ABOUT THAT PERSON:
† NAME OF THE PERSON YOU'RE VOTING FOR:
† WHAT YOU LIKE ABOUT THAT PERSON:
KAZUHITO KAMIYA
Eh...

CHAPTER 31:
HYDRANGEA ALWAYS BLOOM IN THE RAIN

I'll vote for you if you give me a snack, okay?
MNCH
Hm?
MNCH
SHFF SHFF
POPCORN
MIRUKO-SENSEI
† NAME OF THE PERSON YOU'RE VOTING FOR:
PARU-KUN
† WHAT YOU LIKE ABOUT THAT PERSON:
So cute!
I talk with him every now and then.
LOVE.
† NAME OF THE PERSON YOU'RE VOTING FOR:
Senri-sensei
† WHAT YOU LIKE ABOUT THAT PERSON:
He's hot.
I dream about having a date with him by the sea at sunset.
CHOKO-SENSEI
I'm the best-looking teacher at Imperial Academy. Nice to meet you.
TEE HEE HEE

Chapter 31: Hydrangea Always Bloom in the Rain

Lead-in

Haine's wish. Ushio's feelings.
Two hearts melt together as one...

I'm giving away the story!

This is the chapter of the enraged Ushio! (I really like the lead-in my supervisor came up with.) I put the most effort into the scene with Maora and Ushio. Mao-chan is pretending to be tough, but he's actually pretty shocked. He's easygoing, but he's also very delicate...

The scene with Haine and Senri is an important scene too. When you see the close-up of Senri's eyes—that's clearly a look of jealousy toward Haine. You know, jealousy. He must have been a little irritated with her. It's a "why don't you think for yourself" look. But he's not going to take responsibility for Ushio... What a terrible guy!

Yuki-chan is in an interesting position so I'd like to try and have him appear again in later chapters.

BUT...
...I LOVE SHIZUMASA-SAMA TOO.
THESE ARE MY...
...TRUE FEELINGS.
I'M REALLY CONFUSED RIGHT NOW...
I THOUGHT IF I TOLD YOU THIS...
...I'D HURT YOU...
...SO I COULDN'T SAY ANYTHING.
BUT MY HEART BEATS SO FAST WHEN I'M WITH YOU, TAKANARI-SAMA....
...AND IT MAKES ME WANT TO GET CLOSER TO YOU...

...IT'S LONELY FOR ME...
...TO JUST WATCH YOU...
YOU'VE ALWAYS THOUGHT THAT SHIZUMASA AND I WERE THE SAME PERSON.
I CAN'T BE UPSET THAT YOUR FEELINGS ARE SPLIT INTO TWO AFTER LEARNING THAT WE'RE ACTUALLY TWINS.
I DON'T BLAME YOU AT ALL.
THEN IT'S OKAY?
Eh?
HUH?

SHOCK
OF COURSE NOT!
SO YOU BETTER HURRY UP...
...AND BECOME MINE.
UNTIL THEN...
...I'LL BEHAVE LIKE A GENTLEMAN.
B-BMP

THAT'S LOVE, ISN'T IT?
PLEASE, GOD...
BUT THERE'S A FEELING INSIDE ME THAT STILL WANTS THEM BOTH TO HOLD ME...
IN THE END, THERE'S ONLY ONE PERSON FOR ME...
I'M NOT ALLOWED TO BE IN LOVE WITH BOTH OF THEM.
SO ULTIMATELY, I WILL END UP HURTING ONE OF THEM.
KRAK

I'm sorry, Nee-sama. Nee-sama!
??
I'm so glad you're okay.
I'm sorry you were injured...

WHAT?
USHIO IS ABSENT FROM SCHOOL AGAIN TODAY?!
ZZT
OW!
GLOM
I WENT TO HER HOUSE...
...BUT SHE DOESN'T ANSWER THE DOOR.
I WONDER WHAT'S WRONG? SHE'S NEVER DONE THIS BEFORE.
THE STUDENT COUNCIL MEMBERS AT THEIR MORNING MEETING BEFORE CLASS
IT'S BEEN THREE DAYS NOW.
DID YOU TEXT HER?
KA-CHAK
I DID, BUT SHE HASN'T REPLIED.
She's turned off her cell.

KYAH! A TENDER SCENE! ♡
Aah!
TAKANARI-SAMA...
...IS MUCH MORE CARING THAN BEFORE.
What was that?
ARE YOU OKAY?
Be careful.
OF COURSE.
Y-YES...
I LOVE HER!
OH
B-BMP

WHY ARE YOU BLUSHING, MAGURI?!
You've got Mao-chan!
IT'S BECAUSE HE'S A FLIRT!
Listen, Haine-chan...
BUT SHIZUN...
...IS SO CUTE!
It's love.
HEH HEH HEH
I'M JUST ACTING GENTLE-MANLY...
SO SHE IS AT SCHOOL TODAY. ☆
She just didn't come to our meeting, that's all.
THAT'S TAMIYA-KUN, ISN'T IT?
I WONDER WHAT THEY'RE DOING?
!!
AH! I JUST SAW USHIO-CHAN!!
Outside.
HUH?! REALLY?!

UH...
SILENCE
SO USHIO IS GOING OUT WITH TAMIYA-KUN, I GUESS!!
HA HA HA HA
I DIDN'T KNOW THAT!
BUT AT ORIENTATION SHE—
SHE NEVER TOLD ME...
Hmph!
THAT'S A SURPRISE!
HAINE.

SHE DIDN'T TELL ME.
YOU NEVER SAID ANY-THING...
I DIDN'T KNOW.
USHIO.
SO YOU HAVEN'T TALKED TO HAINE-CHAN...
...AT ALL, HUH.

I'M HAINE-CHAN'S FRIEND!
IT IS MY BUSINESS!
IT'S NONE OF YOUR BUSINESS.
AND I'M YOUR FRIEND TOO...
...USHIO-CHAN.
YOU DON'T KNOW ANYTHING!
YOU HYPOCRITE!
WHAT?
NOW YOU PRETEND TO BE KIND TO OTHERS TO SHOW OFF HOW HAPPY YOU ARE?!
STOP TRYING TO IMPOSE YOUR IDIOTIC DO-GOODISM ON ME!!

I...
...REALLY HATE YOU!!

WH-WHAT...
...JUST HAPPENED?
I GUESS YOU CAN...
...GET ANGRY LIKE EVERYONE ELSE...

TA-DAH
HAINE-SAN! I HAVE A LETTER FOR YOU!
OH. THANK YOU VERY MUCH.
You changed just for this?
IT'S INFORMATION ON USHIO-SAN.
!!
FLUP
Senri-sensei knows everything...
Pen Name: Star Mark ☆Lover
WHY SENRI-SENSEI ?!
DIZZ
DIZZ
DIZZ
AND WHY DID HE HAVE TO COME AS THE POSTMAN ?!
?
AND WHY DOES MAO-CHAN KNOW ABOUT IT?!
SHOCK
IS IT ONLY ME?!
AM I THE ONLY ONE WHO DOESN'T KNOW?

USHIO...
WE'RE FRIENDS, AREN'T WE?
HAS IT ALL COME TO AN END?
ALL I NEED IS YOU, HAINE.
YOUR WORDS...
OH.
TAMIYA-KUN AND AMAMIYA-KUN?
YES, I THINK THEY'RE DATING.

UM, ARE YOU AND USHIO CLOSE?
DOES SHE CONFIDE IN YOU?
TWEET TWEET
HE KNEW RIGHT AWAY!
OH, RIGHT...
YES.
SHOCK
But even he still knew about it!!!
Eh?
NOT AT ALL.
THEN...
...HOW DO YOU KNOW...
...SOMETHING LIKE THAT?
CHINK
TAKE THIS.
THIS ISN'T THE PLACE TO DISCUSS IT.

WAIT FOR ME IN THE INFIRMARY.
1F
INFIRMARY
USHIO.
YOU'RE...
...VERY DEAR TO ME.
YOU KNOW HOW FAR I'VE FALLEN INTO THE DARKNESS...
...BUT YOU STILL WATCH OVER ME, HELPING ME MOVE TOWARD THE LIGHT.
...I WANT TO KNOW THAT TOO,
SO IF THERE IS DARKNESS WITHIN YOU, USHIO...

IF YOU DON'T WANT TO TALK ABOUT IT, YOU CAN JUST NOD.
TELL ME THAT YOU NEED ME.
GIVE ME A SIGN AS TO HOW YOU FEEL...
ZWIK
?!
KREEK
HMM...
I GUESS I'LL SIT IN A CHAIR AND WAIT FOR HIM...?
IS THERE SOMEONE HERE?!
MAYBE SOMEONE IS ILL?!
BUT SENRI-SENSEI TOLD ME TO WAIT HERE...
WHAT SHOULD I DO?!

HUH?

IF YOU CAN CALL FOOLING AROUND IN THIS ROOM "DATING"...

...THEN AMAMIYA-KUN....

...IS DATING SEVERAL MEN.

When I posted this on my blog, my supervisor sent me all the volumes.

(>_<)^ Thank you very much!

HAINE ?!
UM.
USHIO?
ARE YOU SEEING YUKIMITSU-SAN TOO?
DASH
USHIO!
USHIO-SAN?!
GRR
SMIRK

TMP TMP TMP

WAIT, USHIO!

USHIO!!

ABANDONED

...

GLARE

Hey, there...

BLAME OTOMIYA-KUN IF YOU HAVE TO...

DON'T BLAME ME.

I wasn't the one who interrupted you two.

HUFF
HUFF
HUFF
USHIO!
IS IT TRUE THAT YOU'RE DATING...
...A LOT OF GUYS AT ONCE?!
SINCE WHEN?!
USHIO, WAIT!!
...
USHIO... I THOUGHT YOU DIDN'T LIKE MEN.
SINCE...
...I ENTERED HIGH SCHOOL.
I'M NOT LIKE YOU, HAINE.

EVEN IF I HATE THEM...
...I DON'T CARE IF THEY DO STUFF TO ME.
BUT THAT'S WRONG!
YOU SHOULDN'T DO THAT!
UNLESS IT'S WITH SOMEONE YOU REALLY LOVE...
...YOU SHOULDN'T DO THINGS LIKE THAT!
WHAT'S WRONG, USHIO?
YOU'RE LIKE A TOTAL STRANGER TO ME.
SO...
WHY...
SHUT UP!

IF I STOPPED ...
WOULD YOU STAY WITH ME ALL THE TIME?!
HUH?

THUD
?!
USHIO?!
WHY...?
I HATE MEN! I HATE THEM ALL!
AND I DON'T WANT...
...TO BE FRIENDS WITH OTHER GIRLS EITHER!
I...

...NEED ONLY YOU, HAINE.
I WANT TO BREAK HER.
I WANT TO BREAK HER.
I WANT TO BREAK HER.
HER SMILE, PURITY, EVERY-THING...
I WANT TO BREAK HAINE APART.

IF I'M NOT...
...THE MOST IMPORTANT PERSON TO YOU...
IF SHE'S NEVER GOING TO BECOME MINE...
THEN I NEVER WANT TO SEE YOU AGAIN.
HAINE, IF...
...YOU DON'T FEEL THE SAME WAY...

JUST...
...STAY THE HELL AWAY FROM ME!!
CHAPTER 31/END

† NAME OF THE PERSON YOU'RE VOTING FOR:
Komaki, of course!!
† WHAT YOU LIKE ABOUT THAT PERSON:
I just suddenly realized how much I like her.
Really...!!
ARINA TANEMURA
Hmph.
...anything to appeal.
I don't have...
PHFF PHFF
Hi, it's me, Arina.
Senri here.
Je t'aime.

CHAPTER 32: REMINISCENCE, THE CANARY'S SONG

THE GENTLEMEN'S ALLIANCE CROSS

It's absolutely intolerable for a mere butler like you to appear in the poll twice...!
Komaki
You should draw Nee-sama! Nee-sama, I say!
HA HA HA
HA HA HA
I agree...

Chapter 32: Reminiscence, the Canary's Song

Lead-in Will there ever be a day when we can smile again...?

I'm giving away the story!

I've finally been able to throw in the Heretics again...but there's one thing I noticed... Haine tends to become rather menacing when I have her interact with the Heretic members... Maybe the Yanki inside awakens?! Well, it's funny, so I enjoy it a lot. (laugh)

A friend of mine asked, "Who got the notebook ready for the exchange diary?!" I'd like to answer that here! Yuki-chan went to buy it himself. (The Heretics tailed him and watched over him from afar.)

I put a lot of effort into the scene with Haine and Mao-chan. Maybe I favor Mao-chan? (Or it could be that he's easy to draw and include in the story?)

The phrase, "If Ushio is to have a new friend..." is a very complex one for Haine. When she said it, about 80 percent of her feelings were against it. Basically, Haine-chan's feelings for Ushio are as strong as Ushio's for her, and she really wants to be Ushio's one and only friend. But she knows that it wouldn't be good for Ushio, so she's forcing herself to say so. Mao-chan understands this. Ah, friendship... By the way, it's also taboo for the main character to get a haircut during the series, but I've broken that rule too. Haine-chan seems like the docile type, but she can be rather reckless at times...

WOULD YOU STAY WITH ME ALL THE TIME?!
SIGH
IF I STOPPED...
DAMN IT...
THEY'RE LAUGHING AT ME.
I think
HA HA HA
BAH!!
HA HA HA HA HA HA
HOW CUTE!
HOW CUTE!
Itsuki-san! You shouldn't laugh about it...
HEE HEE HEE
WHAT SHOULD I DO? USHIO IS GOING TO LEAVE ME...
JUST STAY THE HELL AWAY FROM ME!!
BUT IF I TOLD HER THAT...
THEN I NEVER WANT TO SEE YOU AGAIN.
USHIO IS VERY DEAR TO ME...
I DON'T SEE HER THAT WAY...
...AREN'T WE FRIENDS?!

USHIO WILL LEAVE ME...
WHAT SHOULD I DO?
DO YOU FEEL LIKE EATING SOME-THING?
HOW DO YOU FEEL, HAINE-CHAN?
KNOK KNOK
TUP
...HAS A GIRL EVER HAD A CRUSH ON YOU?
RYOKKA-SAN...
TUP
AS IN LOVE!!
Eh? AS IN LOVE?!
B-BMP
Please tell me
BUT IT'S A GOOD THING TO BE CUTE!!
OH?! WELL... WE'RE SORRY.
YOU GUYS WERE LAUGHING AT ME, WEREN'T YOU...?

HERE, PLEASE USE THIS HANDKERCHIEF.
ARE YOU OKAY?
Oh.
Have some water.
IT'S NOT UNUSUAL FOR GIRLS IN THEIR EARLY ADOLESCENCE, IS IT?
MAIKA-SAMA....
I never told her my feelings, though.
SMILE
NO, IT WAS THE OTHER WAY AROUND. ♥
KOFF
KOFF KOFF
I ALWAYS KEPT IT A SECRET...
...BUT I REALLY ADORED HER.
WHAT ABOUT YOU, HAINE-CHAN?
DO YOU LOVE THIS GIRL TOO?
Um...
NOT IN THAT WAY.
YES...
BUT...

BUT...
...SHE'S A VERY DEAR...
...FRIEND TO ME!
THE TRUTH WILL PROBABLY HURT HER...
...BUT YOUR FRIENDSHIP FOR HER...
...WILL SURELY HELP HEAL THOSE WOUNDS.
THEN...
...IT'LL BE FINE.

YOU'LL BE ABLE TO BECOME EVEN BETTER FRIENDS WITH HER...
...AS LONG AS YOU DON'T GIVE UP, HAINE-CHAN.
SHOVE
OOOH!
IT MAY NOT SEEM LIKE IT, BUT I AM TRYING, YOU KNOW... ♡
OOF!
WOW, RYOKKA-SAN.
HUH?
PLIP PLIP
YOU REALLY SOUND LIKE MY MOTHER.

THANK YOU...
...RYOKKA-SAN.
WITNESSED THE SCENE
MOVED
DEEPLY MOVED
NO MATTER WHAT, I HAVE TO TALK TO HER AGAIN!!
USHIO!!
DO WHAT?!
We should do that too!
KUSAME-KUN!!
No way!
One of my male fans told me that I'm a tsundere.
Minase
Your self-portrait is obviously "tsun" anyway.
HMPH

I BET USHIO SKIPPED SCHOOL AGAIN TODAY.
MAYBE I'LL DROP BY HER HOUSE ON THE WAY HOME.
TA-DAH!
HOLD IT RIGHT THERE!!
HEY, GIRL!!
YOU WANNA JOIN ME FOR A DRINK SOME-WHERE?
MORNING, MAGURI.
I'm still sleepy...
WOO! NO COMMENT.
OH
WHAT DO YOU WANT?
UH... UM.
BLUSH
"I went a little too far with the "woo."
SHK SHK
I GET IT!

USHIO
MAORA
EMPEROR
NO WAY!!
But, I'm really jealous of the first two kisses!!
That's disgusting! You're sick! I can't believe you!
YOU'VE COME TO STEAL A KISS FROM ME NOW THAT YOU'RE THE ONLY ONE IN THE STUDENT COUNCIL WHO HASN'T, RIGHT...?!
OH MY...
WHAT ARE MEMBERS OF THE SCHOOL DISCIPLINE COMMITTEE DOING HERE?
VMP
AT ANY RATE, YOU'RE COMING WITH ME, OTOMIYA !!
COME OUT, HERETICS!!
WHY ARE YOU PUTTING ON A MASK?!
PHEW... I WAS SCARED THERE FOR A SEC.
OH, I GUESS YOU'RE RIGHT.

GWAR
I'M SORRY, PLATINUM!!
PLEASE COME WITH US!!
GWAR
GWAR
GA
YOU TAKE ONE MORE STEP...
...AND I'LL HAVE YOU KICKED OFF THE DISCIPLINE COMMITTEE.
RE
ACCEPTS ALL CHALLENGES
BAM!
BAM!
SOB SOB
SHE'S OPPRESSING US WITH HER AUTHORITY...
SOB SOB
THE PEN REALLY IS MIGHTIER THAN THE SWORD...
And we asked politely too!
WAH!
WAH!
WAH!
Are they okay?
YUKIMITSU-SAN WANTS TO TALK TO ME, RIGHT?! JUST TAKE ME TO HIM!!
Oh please!

BAMM!
Tsujimiya Clan
Oh.
SO YOUR FAMILY REALLY IS IN THE YAKUZA.
BLUSH
SHUT UP!
COME ON, I'LL TAKE YOU TO NII-CHAN!!
GLARE
What do you want?
HUH? SHE'S A FRIEND OF THE YOUNG MASTER?
SHE LOOKS SO FRAIL.
I HEARD SHE'S A MEMBER OF THE STUDENT COUNCIL.
OI, DON'T YOU GUYS STARE AT HER!!
DOOM
I may have quit, but I'm still the Hama Cinderella.
Don't you stare at me, damn it!
WHOA, SHE REALLY IS A FRIEND OF THE YOUNG MASTER!
SHE AIN'T NO ORDINARY GIRL!!

THOP
YOU'RE A MEMBER OF THE DISCIPLINE COMMITTEE, SO YOU'RE NOT SUPPOSED TO DITCH SCHOOL!
HMPH
UH...
HELLO, OTOMIYA-KUN.
WELCOME.
OH?
WHERE ARE MY BOYS?
The Heretics
WOULD YOU GET TO THE POINT?
URGH
Gheesh
I WANTED TO APOLOGIZE FOR THAT LITTLE TRYST BETWEEN USHIO-SAN AND MYSELF—
AAAH! EX-YANKI!!
HA-HA-HA
They shouldn't pick a fight with me!
I TIED THEM UP AND THREW THEM INTO THE POND.
WARGH!
Eeek!
Yukimitsu-sama!
SPLSH
SPLSH

I'D LIKE YOU...
...TO FIRMLY REJECT USHIO-SAN.
I KNOW SHE HAS FEELINGS...
...OF UNREQUITED LOVE TOWARDS YOU.
AND THERE WERE TIMES...
...WHEN I FELT THAT I SHOULDN'T SAY ANYTHING ABOUT IT AS LONG AS SHE WAS HAPPY, BUT...
CHAK
WHAT'S THIS NOTE-BOOK?
AN EXCHANGE DIARY BETWEEN USHIO-SAN AND MYSELF!!

Well...
SHE DOESN'T HAVE A PET BIRD, DOES SHE?
USHIO KEEPS TALKING ABOUT A BIRD IN ALL HER ENTRIES...
USHIO-SAN, YOU'RE SO BEAUTI
...
11/30
USHIO →
The canary seems to have the blues.
At lunch time, the canary ate less than half of
yet, the canary
singing so sadly
the canary smiling
close to
Oh...
FLIP
HE THOUGHT HAINE WAS GOING TO MAKE FUN OF HIM.
NO...
I THINK THE CANARY IS SUPPOSED TO BE YOU.
...ALL THE ENTRIES SHE WROTE WERE ABOUT YOU.
WHEN I ASKED HER TO WRITE ANYTHING SHE WANTED IN THE DIARY...
The canary has been set free by its master, but she was crying in the rain.
I'm sad to see the canary cry.
...
I don't understand why the canary fancies such a man.
I hate him.
...but inside, a part of me was happy. I couldn't go near with that feeling of guilt.
I wanted to speak to her...

But it's fine.

As long as the canary doesn't have her feelings returned...

...I can listen to her songs with a peaceful mind.

FLUP

The canary is kind to everyone.

The canary shares her smiles with everyone.

And at times like that, I feel a strong hatred inside me, making me want to capture the canary.

But...

When I think that the canary is just being kind to me, like she is with everyone...
...my heart hurts so much I can't speak.
I want you to see the real me.
No, that's not true. I don't want you to know anything about it.
When your heart finally reaches someone...
...which will I choose?
The sword...
...or the shield?

YOU IDIOT...
USHIO.
LOVE IS SUPPOSED TO BE SOMETHING FUN, RIGHT?
I'M GLAD TO HAVE FALLEN IN LOVE WITH SHIZUMASA-SAMA, AND I'M HAPPY TO BE IN LOVE WITH TAKANARI-SAMA.
WHAT ABOUT YOU, USHIO?
...REVEALS YOUR TORMENT.
I NEED TO GET GOING.
OTOMIYA-KUN!!
EVERY-THING YOU'VE WRITTEN HERE...
CAN YOU TELL ME THAT YOU'RE HAPPY TO BE IN LOVE WITH ME?

PLEASE, OTOMIYA-KUN!!
YOU HAVE TO MAKE USHIO-SAN GIVE UP ON YOU!!
I CAN'T GIVE YOU AN ANSWER RIGHT NOW.
IF ONLY I WERE YOU!!
SHOCK
WHY DOES IT HAVE TO BE YOU?!
IF I WERE YOU...
...I WOULD BE ABLE TO MAKE USHIO-SAN HAPPY!

TO HELL WITH THAT!!
IT'S USHIO'S RESPONSIBILITY TO FIND HER OWN HAPPINESS!!

I'M SURE THAT THERE'S SOMETHING THAT ONLY YOU CAN DO.
HUH? YOU'VE ALREADY FINISHED TALKING?
I BROUGHT SOME TEA...
MAGURI BEING NICE
WHAT SHOULD I DO, MAGU-MAGU?
DON'T YOU RUN AWAY FROM LOOKING FOR THAT...
...SENPAI!
I SEEM TO HAVE...
...HURT OTOMIYA-KUN'S FEELINGS.

I SHOULD HAVE KNOWN...
...THAT SHE WISHES FOR USHIO-SAN'S HAPPINESS AS MUCH AS I DO.
I...
IT'S NOT FOR ME TO BRING HAPPINESS TO USHIO.
...CAN ONLY...
WHAT THE HELL?!!
WHAT THE HELL? WHAT THE HELL?!
HAINE!
HAINE-CHAN!!
I'M GLAD YOU'RE HERE.
I WAS WORRIED SINCE MAGURI AND AMAMIYA HAVEN'T SHOWN UP EITHER.
SLP
WHAT'S THE MATTER?
EMPEROR...

I'M RETURNING...
...YOUR RIBBON.
I...
...CAN NO LONGER BE..
...YOUR PLATINUM.

KA-CHAK
BOW
HAINE-CHAN!!
HAINE-CHAN, YOU CAN'T BE SERIOUS?!

WHY ARE YOU BREAKING IT OFF?!
HEY!
LISTEN TO ME!!
Gehh!
MAO-CHAN...
...DO YOU LIKE USHIO?
YES.
BUT, USHIO-CHAN....
...SAID SHE HATED ME...
DON'T TAKE THAT TO HEART, MAO-CHAN!!
YOU STILL TRY TO TALK TO USHIO, DON'T YOU?!

YOU STILL TRY TO TELL HER...
...HOW YOU FEEL, RIGHT?
HATE ISN'T A FEELING THAT GOES ON FOREVER!
YOU NEVER KNOW WHEN SHE'LL CHANGE HER MIND...
PLEASE...
...DON'T GIVE UP.
TRY TO GET TO USHIO'S HEART.
HAINE-CHAN.

IF...
...USHIO IS TO HAVE A NEW FRIEND...
...I WANT IT TO BE YOU, MAO-CHAN.
OKAY.
OKAY.
I'LL KEEP TRYING.

ANYWAY, OPEN THE DOOR!
USHIO?
I EMAILED YOU THREE TIMES, YOU KNOW...
Hmph.
I NEED TO TALK TO YOU.
...
HAINE?!
BAM

I WANTED...
...TO GIVE YOU MY TIE.

HAINE.
YOUR HAIR...
LET'S START OVER FROM THAT DAY AGAIN...
THAT DAY WHEN WE LEFT MIDDLE SCHOOL...
I'M YOURS, USHIO.
YOU'RE THE MOST IMPORTANT PERSON TO ME.

NOBODY ELSE CAN DO THIS...

THE GENTLEMEN'S ALLIANCE † 7/END

THE GENTLEMEN'S ALLIANCE CROSS

BONUS FUNNIES

WELL DRAWN
KRRK
P-PLEASE DRAW ME!!
NOW IT'S HAINE-CHAN'S TURN! ♡♡
Ooh!
Hee.
SORRY, BUT I'M A LITTLE TIRED.

EVEN TO SHIZUN?!
DONE.
FLUP

TOO BAD.
He's shy about drawing you...
OH.
I'M GOING TO GO TAKE A WALK.
TMP TMP

SHIZUN, WHAT ABOUT ME?! DO ME!
IN THE ZONE
IT'S A PRETTY REALISTIC PORTRAIT OF USHIO-CHAN, ISN'T IT?
Me! Me! Me! Me!

I love you!
FLUP

DONE.
Blond hair
Ear
Tail
Smiley
Soft
Grass
FLUP

STARE
Uh-huh. Uh-huh.

IT'S CUTE, BUT HE'S A PET!!
IT'S CUTE, BUT HE'S A PET!!
YUP.
TH-THIS IS WHAT I LOOK LIKE TO YOU?
BLUSH

THE GENTLEMEN'S ALLIANCE CROSS
BONUS STORY: MAORA'S MIND ORACLE GENERATION
DAD, MOM...
WE'RE GOING TO GET MARRIED!!
HA HA HA HA! YOSHITAKA! BOYS CAN'T MARRY EACH OTHER!
HA
HA
HA
BOYS HAVE TO MARRY GIRLS!!
HA
HA
HA
HA
BAH

AFTER THAT, MAGURI STOPPED TALKING TO ME.
THEY USED TO PLAY TOGETHER EVERY DAY...
I FEEL RESPONSIBLE TOO.
MA! ORA!
THRUP
THRUP
SO? WHAT'S HE DOING NOW?
TRANSFORM INTO A VOLUPTUOUS OFFICE LADY! ☆
Lovely!
Find the Miracle Peach inside your heart!
MIND ORACLE GENERATION!!
THE MAGIC SPELL FROM THE ANGEL WARRIOR ANIME?
I guess he can't pronounce the entire spell yet.
HE WANTS TO TURN INTO A GIRL!
OKAY, YOSHITA-KACCHI!
DADDY WILL HELP YOU!!
WOW!
Really?
BUT!

ONE MONTH LATER...
MAGURI!!
MA! ORA!!
DON'T FORGET TO SAY THE MAGIC SPELL WHEN YOU WANT TO TRANS-FORM!!
This can't be good.
GOOD WORK! YOU'RE SO CUTE!!
But a little dumb.
GLOMP
HURRAY!
You know, like makeup and girly talk...
I PRAC-TICED EVERY DAY...
...AND NOW I'M A GIRL!!

SORRY...
...BUT I LIKE BOYS.
BOYS?
After all I've done?!
WHAT THE...?!
HUH?
Ah.
He's my type.
TMP TMP

BUT IF YOU STOPPED WEARING THINGS LIKE THAT...
...AND LOOKED LIKE A BOY, I'D CONSIDER MAYBE GOING OUT WITH YOU.
I'LL...
...NEVER GO OUT WITH YOU!!!
FWAK!!
GRIP
?
I'LL...
I'LL...
EVER SINCE THEN I'VE KEPT ON FIGHTING WITH MAGURI.
AND I'VE WILLFULLY MAINTAINED MY "FEMININITY."

THE NICKNAME MY FATHER GAVE ME AS A JOKE...
...SPREAD AMONG MY FRIENDS...
...AND WON'T DISA-PPEAR.
JUST LIKE THAT FEELING I GOT THAT DAY...
...WHEN I DECIDED...
...TO MARRY HIM.

ILLUSTRATIONS
Various illustrations.
In other words, scribbles.
They're all Hainekko.

NOTES ON THE TEXT

PAGE 6:

"This is a one-shot, which is rare for *The Gentleman's Alliance †*."
A "one-shot" is a story that starts and concludes in one chapter. The literal term is *ichiwa kanketsu*, which means "one episode conclusive style."

"I tried drawing her in a mini form…"
Tanemura-sensei is talking about a *mini-kyara*, or "mini character."

PAGE 11:

Animal Crossing
Animal Crossing, or *Doubutsu no Mori*, is an interactive game in which the player leads a virtual life in "real time." Your friends can also visit you in the game. You can go fishing, shopping, grow vegetables, etc.

PAGE 12:

"A stray cat with a fish in his mouth..."
Osakana kuwaeta doraneko seems to be a classical theme in Japan. Since the Japanese consume a lot of fish, in the old days stray cats were known for stealing fish from the fishmongers.

PAGE 43:

Moe
Moe is an otaku term meaning a strong love or fetish for something or someone—usually manga, anime, or game characters.

PAGE 51:

Karuta Tournament

Karuta is a Japanese card game. The name itself is from the Portuguese word *carta*, or "card". There are several versions of the game, but usually the cards are split into "reading cards" and "illustration cards." Each illustration card has a letter written on it from the Japanese alphabet (in hiragana). Someone will read out the contents of the reading card, and the goal of the players is to find the matching illustration card. There is a letter in the corner of the illustration card that coincides with the first letter of the sentence being read out, so the players are able to look for the right card from the moment the reading card is read out loud. The aim of the game is to collect as many illustration cards as possible and to have the highest number of cards at the end. Karuta cards are extremely large (as you can see from Ushio carrying them).

Shinji and Natsuki

Shinji and Natsuki are characters from *Kamikaze Kaito Jeanne*. Shinji is the rebirth of Access, and he is Miyako and Yamato's son. Natsuki is the rebirth of Fin, and she is the daughter of Maron and Chiaki.

Maroyan

"Maroyan" is Tanemura-sensei's nickname for Maron—the main character in *Jeanne*.

PAGE 53:

Bamboo Group roll call...

Although some schools in Japan have classroom name designations rather than number, this is probably just a group name for the orientation and not an actual classroom name.

PAGE 81:

Arina Nikki

Arina Nikki is the name of the blog.

MM Boys

This is an abbreviation for "Maguri Maora Boys."

PAGE 141:

Exchange Diary

An exchange diary is a diary or notebook shared between friends who write entries and comments. Exchange diaries were pretty popular among girls in elementary and middle schools in the 1990s.

PAGE 143:

"Do you feel like eating something?"

Ryokka-san made Haine *zousui*, which is soupy rice.

PAGE 147:

Tsundere

Tsundere is an otaku term for girls who tend to be rather unfriendly or prickly at first, but are gentle, loving, and kind once you get to know them. The word is a combination of *tsunsun*, or "prickly, morose" and *dere dere*, or "lovestruck."

PAGE 151:

Nii-chan

Nii-chan means "older brother."

"Don't you stare at me, damn it!"

Literally this is *menchi o kiru*, a yanki term meaning "to give someone the eye."

PAGE 160:

Senpai

Senpai means "senior." It refers to someone older than the speaker. Many students call students who are older than they are "Senpai." In this case, Haine is using it to reprimand Yukimitsu—normally she refers to him as "Yukimitsu-san."

PAGE 175:

"Transform into a voluptuous office lady!"

In the Japanese, she also says *bon kyu bon*, which is "bam, squeeze, bam!" It is slang used to talk about women with big boobs, small waists, and large hips.

"Find the Miracle Peach inside your heart!"

This is a play on the Japanese tongue-twister *sumomo mo momo mo momo no uchi*, meaning "the word *momo* can be found in both *sumomo* (plum) and *momo* (peach)."

The student council members started to get along gradually, so recently it's been a joy to draw them. A while ago, they tended to be very individualistic, but now they have become closer friends and naturally interfere with each other. I feel like a headmaster watching over them (I don't exactly feel like a parent to them). Anyway, the Ushio arc has begun, and another big wave is heading toward them!

—*Arina Tanemura*

Arina Tanemura was born in Aichi, Japan. She got her start in 1996, publishing *Nibanme no Koi no Katachi* (The Style of the Second Love) in *Ribon Original* magazine. Her early work includes a collection of short stories called *Kanshaku Dama no Yuutsu* (Short-Tempered Melancholic). Two of her titles, *Kamikaze Kaito Jeanne* and *Full Moon*, were made into popular TV series. Tanemura enjoys karaoke and is a huge *Lord of the Rings* fan.

THE GENTLEMEN'S ALLIANCE† vol.7

The Shojo Beat Manga Edition

STORY & ART BY
ARINA TANEMURA

English Translation & Adaptation/Tetsuichiro Miyaki
Touch-up Art & Lettering/George Caltsoudas
Design/Amy Martin
Editor/Nancy Thistlethwaite

Editor in Chief, Books/Alvin Lu
Editor in Chief, Magazines/Marc Weidenbaum
VP of Publishing Licensing/Rika Inouye
VP of Sales/Gonzalo Ferreyra
Sr. VP of Marketing/Liza Coppola
Publisher/Hyoe Narita

THE GENTLEMEN ALLIANCE -CROSS- © 2004 by Arina Tanemura. All rights reserved. First published in Japan in 2004 by SHUEISHA Inc., Tokyo. English translation rights arranged by SHUEISHA Inc. The stories, characters and incidents mentioned in this publication are entirely fictional.

No portion of this book may be reproduced or transmitted in any form or by any means without written permission from the copyright holders.

The rights of the author(s) of the work(s) in this publication to be so identified have been asserted in accordance with the Copyright, Designs and Patents Act 1988. A CIP catalogue record for this book is available from the British Library.

Printed in Canada

Published by VIZ Media, LLC
P.O. Box 77010
San Francisco, CA 94107

Shojo Beat Manga Edition
10 9 8 7 6 5 4 3 2 1
First printing, September 2008

PARENTAL ADVISORY
THE GENTLEMEN'S ALLIANCE† is rated T+ for Older Teen and is recommended for ages 16 and up. This volume contains suggestive themes.
ratings.viz.com

Arina Tanemura Series

The Gentlemen's Alliance †

Haine Otomiya joins Imperial Academy in pursuit of the boy she's loved since she was a child, unaware that he has many secrets of his own.

I•O•N

Chanting the letters of her first name has always brought Ion Tsuburagi good luck—but her good-luck charm is really the result of psychic powers!

Full Moon

Mitsuki Koyama dreams of becoming a pop star, but she is dying of throat cancer. Can she live out a lifetime of dreams in just one year?

Short-Tempered Melancholic

A collection of short stories including Arina Tanemura's debut manga, "In the Style of the Second Love"!

Time Stranger Kyoko

Kyoko Suomi must find 12 holy stones and 12 telepaths to awaken her sister who has been trapped in time since birth.

THE GENTLEMEN ALLIANCE -CROSS- © 2004 by Arina Tanemura/SHUEISHA Inc. I·O·N © 1997 by Arina Tanemura/SHUEISHA Inc. FULLMOON-WO SAGASHITE © 2001 by Arina Tanemura/SHUEISHA Inc. KANSHAKUDAMA NO YUUTSU © 1998 by Arina Tanemura/SHUEISHA Inc. TIME STRANGER KYOKO © 2000 by Arina Tanemura/SHUEISHA Inc.

Turn Back the Clock

In the 30th century, Kyoko Suomi is the princess of Earth—but she wants absolutely nothing to do with the throne! In order to get out of her royal responsibilities, she'll have to travel through time to find her long-lost twin. Will Kyoko locate her missing sister, or will she end up as Earth's reluctant ruler?

Find out in *Time Stranger Kyoko*—manga on sale now!

Shojo Beat Manga
Time Stranger Kyoko
Arina Tanemura

Time Stranger Kyoko

By Arina Tanemura, creator of *Full Moon*, *The Gentlemen's Alliance†* and *I•O•N*

On sale at:
www.shojobeat.com
Also available at your local bookstore and comic store

Shojo Beat MANGA from the HEART

RATED T+ FOR OLDER TEEN ratings.viz.com

viz media
www.viz.com

TIME STRANGER KYOKO © 2000 by Arina Tanemura/SHUEISHA Inc.

Currently serialized in Shojo Beat *magazine – from the creator of* MeruPuri

VAMPIRE KNIGHT™

By Matsuri Hino

Cross over to the night..

Cross Academy is attende
by two groups of students: th
Day Class and the Night Clas
Yuki Cross and Zero Kiryu a
the Guardians of the schoo
there to protect the Day Clas
from the Academy's dark secre
the Night Class is fu
of vampi

Shojo Beat Manga
VAMPIRE KNIGHT
Story & Art by
Matsuri Hino
1

Only $8.99

Shojo Beat™
MANGA from the HEART

On sale at:
www.shojobeat.com
Also available at your local bookstore and comic store.

Vampire Knight © Matsuri Hino 2004/HAKUSENSHA, Inc.

www.viz.com

FULL MOON WO SAGASHITE © 2001 by Arina Tanemura/SHUEISHA Inc.
Fushigi Yûgi: Genbu Kaiden © 2004 Yuu WATASE/Shogakukan Inc.
Ouran Koko Host Club © Bisco Hatori 2002/HAKUSENSHA, Inc.

Save OVER 50% off the cover price!

Shojo Beat

MANGA from the HEART

The Shojo Manga Authority

This monthly magazine is injected with the most **ADDICTIVE** shojo manga stories from Japan. PLUS, unique editorial coverage on the arts, music, culture, fashion, and much more!

☑ **YES!** Please enter my one-year subscription (12 GIANT issues) to ***Shojo Beat*** at the LOW SUBSCRIPTION RATE of **$34.99!**

Over 300 pages per issue!

NAME

ADDRESS

CITY STATE ZIP

E-MAIL ADDRESS P7GNC1

☐ MY CHECK IS ENCLOSED (PAYABLE TO *Shojo Beat*) ☐ BILL ME LATER

CREDIT CARD: ☐ VISA ☐ MASTERCARD

ACCOUNT # EXP. DATE

SIGNATURE

CLIP AND MAIL TO

SHOJO BEAT
Subscriptions Service Dept.
P.O. Box 438
Mount Morris, IL 61054-0438

Canada price for 12 issues: $46.99 USD, including GST, HST and QST. US/CAN orders only. Allow 6-8 weeks for delivery. Must be 16 or older to redeem offer. By redeeming this offer I represent that I am 16 or older.

Vampire Knight © Matsuri Hino 2004/HAKUSENSHA, Inc. Nana Kitade © Sony Music Entertainment (Japan), Inc.
CRIMSON HERO © 2002 by Mitsuba Takanashi/SHUEISHA Inc.

RATED T FOR OLDER TEEN
ratings.viz.com

Shojo Beat™

MANGA from the HEART

The Shojo Manga Authority

12 GIANT issues for ONLY $34.99*

The most ADDICTIVE shojo manga stories from Japan PLUS unique editorial coverage on the arts, music, culture, fashion, and much more!

That's 51% OFF the cover price!

Subscribe NOW and become a member of the Sub Club!

- **SAVE** 51% OFF the cover price
- **ALWAYS** get every issue
- **ACCESS** exclusive areas of www.shojobeat.com
- **FREE** members-only gifts several times a year

Strictly VIP!

3 EASY WAYS TO SUBSCRIBE!

1) Send in the subscription order form from this book OR
2) Log on to: www.shojobeat.com OR
3) Call 1-800-541-7876

Canada price for 12 issues: $46.99 USD, including GST, HST and QST. US/CAN orders only. Allow 6-8 weeks for delivery. Must be 16 or older to redeem offer. By redeeming this offer I represent that I am 16 or older.
Vampire Knight © Matsuri Hino 2004/HAKUSENSHA, Inc. Nana Kitade © Sony Music Entertainment (Japan), Inc.
SHOJO EVE ★ EVE'S APPLEWORK 24 HOURS © 2007 by Arina Tanemura/SHUEISHA Inc.
CRIMSON HERO © 2002 by Mitsuba Takanashi/SHUEISHA Inc.

www.viz.com